For The Time Being

A Collection of Poetry

Jordan M. Carter

Printed in the United States of America

First Printing, 2020

ISBN 978-0-578-82797-1
Oils & Ivy Publishing
oilsandivypublishing@gmail.com

To my friends and family who supported me, and to those who believe in the magic of our universe.

Part I
Ver

Emergence

What fresh, fresh fruit
is blinding with its juice—
what joy have I found
in dark?

How lovely it is
to have no control,
and no direction
from the stars.

What freedom lies
beyond our grasp,
in subtle, shimmering hues?
What deep black caves
conceal hidden gems
within their navy blues?

How starkly contrasted
in front of the sun
bleeds the moon,
and darkens,
darkens,
darkens,
until it is out of view.

Beginning and End

Dusk—
prayers are spoken
when pink hues are painted
on a sky that has seen so much sadness,
rich and ugly sadness,
with a soul wrecking tone
that holds torture in its reverence.
It's a darkening feeling,
when he will kiss gently your temple,
and swift is the wind when comes the end.
Life is short, you know,
but it is also small
and is snuffed out quickly—
but not by the breeze of the beginning.
And prayers, they go unanswered
consistently
but you drift away ever so contently
with your ears and eyes trained on the
dawn.

C loaked

The night is easily compared to
velvet drapery as it caresses your rosy cheeks.
Its hands are cool and ease your fever,
as it fondles your body with soft and icy finger tips.
Its arms hang loosely by its sides,
until you feel compelled to fall into it—
and the night has dark tendrils to reach and retrieve all
that fall so willingly in love with the dusk.

It Is New

There is moonlight
on the hearth,
with each new breath
it is an emerging creature.

Of my own accord
I paint this new being
as a cosmic wonder
of mundane origin.

Non-corporeal, unbound by
holy sanctity,
the milky limbs rest
transparently upon the altar.

The ground will freeze the night
of its birth—
yet the bloom under the frost
will be wild and strong.

For the Time Being

Be full of wilderness.
be lost, be right—
have a life filled with fruits,
end becoming, be still the light.

Hold the archway,
hold the curtains,
give your wisdom slight,
be wild, end becoming,
be still the light.

Have hands of old,
drink of milk and
melancholy.
Hang your branches low
for the cat, for the crow,
end becoming, harbor the night.

$\mathcal{B}$ecome

Beginnings are worth the mess
if you can stay amazed at the
wreckage of the old
and remember your spirit
sprang forth from the ether
by its own volition.

When We Were Children

Religion,
twisted thistle—
we used to imbibe ourselves
with honey suckle until
our teeth felt loose with
glee.

Like Voices Cutting Through Air

I may be transient,
a spirit tangled in
every strand of your hair.

Somehow, We Must Leave

Linoleum heartbeats
echo down the hallway
as the plaster turns to stone.
Who will we become
when the forest seeks
her revenge on us?

Dayrise

Browned butter
bruised rose
there is something so comforting
in having no path to follow.

Be it out in the woods,
amongst deciduous trees
with bare branches exposing
their nakedness, and yours.

The curve of the sun
awakening over the hill,
spills like a yolk
broken and dripping over tanned legs.

Country Side

She was really a French Riviera
rallied along two marble stones
picking locks, drunk on chardonnay
in the country side—
rolling hills and mothers
envy.

*W*inter Storm

A nor'easter, I pray that the snowfall does not
match those from my childhood—
European blankets of thick, solid ice.
But even the chill that lives without
cannot twice as easily compare to the one
that resides within—
even so, the anticipation drives deep,
yet the snowfall is silent,
somehow still a beast.

Agnes

Agnes swings with effervescence,
Agnes dreams with both eyes closed.
She only listens to the presence
once the mystery unfolds.

Agnes loves a darkened room,
Agnes knows when to light a match.
She feeds the flames until they bloom,
until they shudder, until they catch.

Agnes uses melody,
Agnes hears notes out of tune.
She infuses harmony,
into life, woven by the loom.

Agnes prays unto the moon,
Agnes bathes in pale starlight.
She is sure it is coming soon,
sure as she is tethered to the night.

As It Were

If I could inscribe
love songs
in my fingerprint grooves,
every touch,
and brush,
and graze,
would have purposeful
melody.

Unlike now,
so clumsy—
and quite stiff.

A smooth transition
to philharmonic
ecstasy
might be welcome—
should it not
threaten
to rewrite
my identity.

As it were—
the sentiment
remains.

In The End

Fox in the forest,
dreams in a cage.
Fur on the floorboards,
ripening with age

Iris in a keyhole,
mist in the air.
The clock on the wall says it's
time to not
be there.

She's calling you out
to the edge,
it's a long, long fall but it's better
in the end

It's in the dry leaves,
lying alone and free,
wounded but still breathing
oh so gently

Run wild with the leaves
in your hair,
port stained lips and
blood in the air.

She's calling you out
to the edge
it's a long, long fall but it's better
in the end.

I Am Here

I am on the marble slab,
sculpted clay guided
by rigid bone.
There is no way to
avoid creation,
as the energy I've
harnessed is
ancient
and has never
experienced
mortality,
let alone
emergence.

It Is Here

Be still—
the silence feeds the growing illness
and nourishes
from below.

Be mindful—
as your eyes peel awake,
a dream can begin
to turn somber.

Ushering Her In

Jessamine crawling over Carolina,
sip on Honeysuckle at the root.

Sparkling wine, bees are flying,
be never ending and free of the vine.

Have your ambrosia, drink your wine
take your time,
slow, slow
summer.

Morning

Those who bathe in darkness
become thirsty for the dawn
and reach with golden
fingertips
until the broken twilight folds.

And when it folds, the times slips by
and the wild juniper gives way
to the birds song and flight.

As molten drops encase the sky
so the dance begins—
a cadence unknown to
creatures who show
their last true sentience.

The Fortunate

Oils and ivy
dance on a canvas of gold—
and how it shimmers
and comes to life,
exonerating the old.

A vision forced upon
the fortunate to swallow,
only washed down with
water from our gardens hose,
how lucky to taste the rust—
and still be washed in shimmer.

Fortune Tells

Stumbling, faltering,
blessed to lie down amongst the ragweed
and wake up with a mind clear as
quartz.

Staring, seeking,
enveloping visions seep through the hardwood
and allow every creature within to know the
truth.

Unholy, Leaking,
fortune and favor follow suit to the watchers
and give in to the suitors of wishful
thinking.

*I*dolatry

Crushed petals
weaving heavy brush strokes
into divine paintings of the old gods
that we used to want to become,
this is the place where our passions lie
and take shape within our bellies
yearning to become ripe—

save for a moment the
involvement of this memory,
tucked away in a locket,
an unsewn front pocket—
the last loneliness we will ever feel,
is yet to come
and pass.

Advantage

Mirror ball,
follow through with your last fulfillment
and your first enthrallment.
For the sake of reality,
shake the lights from your frame
and sell the future that you
create.

$\mathcal{S}$ettle

Moonlight and pearlescent,
fluid hues and sparkling waves—
navy love at the base of the sea,
and it's deep as deep can be.

Piercing rays of golden sun,
shimmer fluorescent and coming undone,
morning comes, and dusk, it settles—
behind velvet drapes and stinging nettle.

Transformative

Survivor of broken land—
blackened eyes,
like charcoal,
not yet diamond.

Soul dampened—
not yet soaked through,
and yet
stronger, with tension.

Part II
Aestas

*W*ait

Ash and aster,
thin branches like twigs
dance with the breeze,
morbid and free.

Like seed, I bury my heart
deep in the soil
and am hushed
as I wait
for the bloom.

Creature, Tell Me

Creature, tell me,
how do you breathe
with heavy stones
upon your chest?

With scarred lips
do you stave off the cold—
creature tell me,
do you fear the unknown?

Do you soak in the old,
when your nose bleeds golden,
creature, tell me,
is humanity so bold?

Creature, tell me,
I long to see,
does the old law still reign
over times such as these?

*R*elease

Wild hips,
tender purple traces
of unruly lips.

Feel the summer
trickle down
between your
shoulder blades

and be free to
recognize,

that you bloom like
wild flowers
in spring
when you release
the winter.

*I*t Will Come

One thing I know
is a year of
rotten fruit
means months
of potent wine
to come—

And neighbors that move
can play tricks
on the moon
and we can be
pregnant with glee.

Matrilineal

She carries the
weight
of a life on her back
and shoulders the
bruises
of a futures
design.
Her familial magic
is in its
melting season
ready and willing
to become
ripe.

*B*edding Canvas

Sky's dark,
roots unfold—
and the water is full of life.

Pours down,
soaks through—
the heart is a landing site.

Loaded up,
lovers gold—
shining through the dark.

Curtains back,
velvet sun—
sheets arranged like art.

$\mathcal{I}$t Continues

Straw in our hair—
does it get any better than
moonlight on your breath?

Summer starved air—
chills on the skin of
the land and the hearth.

Broken bones in the dirt—
a testament to time and
change...
This is our lives true wage—
from fragile youth,
to frail
old
age.

*B*oth Sides

Harvest your worth
where the bloom can be felt
and is rooted
in visions of sweet
longing.

Yield the bounty
of your craft,
revered as the
chaos of storms nourished
the crop.

While the rain has
fed the roots,
we must indulge
that it has drowned any
rot
as well.

Only Nights

The best in me does not
concede to the worst in you,
although there is a stiff silence
when the two converge.

Stalling friction amongst
dirty porcelain, I tell myself
this is not a strategy
which should be employed.

The water peers back—
it wants to help, but it
does not know
exactly how.

Growth

There is trauma in rebirth,
reconcile that within your mind.
You should feel the grooves
of uneven regrowth,
but don't let that sully
your garden.

One thing to note:
you don't have to harvest
your crop or your load
until you are ready
to once again sow.

Determination

The intention of her spirit
folds into the universe
as though it were manuka honey
dropping into tea.
Something imperfect,
but sweet and divinely
produced,
introduced to her timeline
by her own accord.
It has been stirred—
and set with determination.
as it pours out, the tea leaves
say nothing loud,
yet they feel of silent
anticipation.

*U*nworldly

Teething babies
baby's breath
breathing softly—
softness kept.
Weeping mother,
mother's debt,
indebted illness
illness crept.

*S*unlight

In fashionable mistrust,
I look to the west to greet the sun
when it is still night.

Ragweed carpets the land
around me, and I cannot get
the air that I need.

And I'm still seeing westerly shadow,
I figured as much.
one day I'll catch her hiding from us.

The Promised Land

Exhaust from your truck
puts a filmy blanket on the pond
and you infuse your words with my hair.
I am all but listless
as your smooth voice speaks life to
blooming flowers.
Fleeting, you are, but intense,
and lush like a forest in Spring.

Classical

Yellow sky,
bad divinity—
Molasses in the morning,
sunrise immortality.

$\mathcal{Y}$outh

Prolific,
pale,
and under a dark radar.

Curly,
lilac toned,
and shy as can be.

Trembling as a branch in a
crippling breeze - can't see,
can't feel,
can't breathe.

Feeling egg shells break under my feet
I'm barely alive,
but can feel my heart beat.

Start poisoning your body young—
& peel like an orange, so ripe in the sun

Your body is sweet, you're hopeful, still sour
waiting for pruning, when you start to flower

and keep your heart off of your flaws—
lest you fall prey to their
beaks, teeth, and claws.

Loving,
Frothy,
and young like the summer in June
Open,
yet heavy,
broken and ready—

It's all about to begin for you soon.

Few

When we were young the frost stuck to the air
drifted hazily through silent dreams—
unaware of the obvious, and unlikely to become prepared.
Moving through corridors, exhilarating and bold,
innovation developed and tested
with new ideas threatening to shine, golden.
A valiant effort to be so askew—
when we were young,
so we were few.

Quickly

Take inventory of
     freckles
          divots
              and rivers
Before they
     fade out
          fill up
              and run dry.

See

Transfixed portals
swirling and blooming within bright perennials—
tamed by lost oracles
and well-nourished vibration.

Unbelonging

Cataclysmic cultivation—
I can't see how this bulb belongs
among the buds
waiting to sprout forth.
From the outside, you couldn't tell—
but what is growing inside this one
will not be able to root itself
in the network of its
company.

What grows when watered from the can does not feel
the same
as what grows when watered by
the storm.

Optional

Divine feminine
Held together by thistle and vine—
A forming of veneer
And bruised blood,
There never was an option
To suffice
But only sacrifice
To sovereign kinghood
Too hollow for substance.

Ebb

Mysterious waters wash upon the bay,
tinted red with the crashing of waves—
and they never stop,
the tides keep rolling in.

Relentless in their integrity,
indefinite in their erosion—
and if you should feel the compulsion,
do not hesitate to let it seep in.

Holy Nights

Spirits of summer
summon the rights of
bloom and fervor
as the sky melts rose to
cornflower—
here is a ritual worth
partaking in,
a saccharine warmth
radiates through the field,
this is home to flesh,
do not venture far.

*C*oast

Salted banks, a crested virtue
of solitude—averted eyes.
I suppose, in the least of ways,
the granular scape of
sparkling beiges is something to
behold,
just as the humming blue
would be
on a clear day.

Childhood

I used to ride to the countryside of France
with my mother, as a child.
Hills carried us to sweet bistros—
bright angels did not compare,
in an hour or so,
back to Baden-Württemberg,
little memories in the countryside of France
and the return to home at last.

Keep Moving

You are not stuck,
you are not trapped.
This is just where you are
right now.

You are not lost,
you are not lapsed.
This is a place where you
don't have to stay.

Part III
Autumnus

Canyon

Neon porcelain,
smooth, silken
and split,
like a canyon.

Small prayers
for handmade religion,
deep soil,
dried up on dancing tongues.

Wasted communion,
wine spilled over bread,
lilted voices
weaving hallelujah with frayed thread.

Equatorial

Peach tree sunsets,
drunk on blue margaritas—
we only ever kiss goodbye.

Orange blush sky,
cotton white sails,
parted—a torn book
against the horizon.

We only ever kiss goodbye.
And sometimes, goodbye is forever
as if it were summer,
just south of the equator.

Impermanence

Stars dance,
careless waltz.
What form
they maintain.

In mountain skies
they turn,
say hello,
and are gone.

Until next time,
they twirl the same.
What comfort they
bring
to those haunted
by impermanence.

Contradictory

It may not be the prettiest flower
that smells so sweet,
or the thinnest branch
which carries the weight.

It may not be the densest cloud
that drops the rain,
or the sharper knife
that harbors the pain.

Ice

Sometimes when the
air is still,
I can taste the cold
and it is bitter.

My lungs are tired
of breathing in your fire,
but I am afraid
that without it

The ice climbing down
my throat
will overtake
my body.

Familial

He is sewn by a woman's arch,
by a curve, deep as is dark.
Protected only by ashes and aster,
left on him by her ancestor's hearts.

*P*sychic

Candles that glow,
frozen wax in the snow—
it is life that tears us apart.

And no psychic feline,
or woman with green eyes,
can truly ever find us at fault.

Simplicity

Magnolia, Birchwood—smell of the pines,
forgiving of land so dry and unkind
a statement of misery, too cold to pronounce—
ears frozen shut, they can't hear a sound.

This is what flesh feels like in this life—
indentations and exhalations.
simple exonerations.

*S*elling

O Lord, O God
there's devils in the stall
tormenting the livestock—
I can't fight them off.

O Lord, O God
there's misfortune from the North,
gliding down from the mountain,
a curse upon my mouth.

O Lord, O God
the land beneath us is dead,
dried out and rotten—
a curse upon my head.

O Lord, O God
an offer extended to me
of dance and of song,
and plenty of food to eat.

O Lord, O God,
should I partake, a fool I'll be
yet from the bleak perspective,
"The flame will nourish thee."

Holy Land

Between two flames
she whispers
incantations,
covert exaltations
of old ones made
new.

She holds hope
like a jagged stone
digging deep
in her palm
as she knows:

A foreign god can't
keep the peace
on stolen land,
and she feels
relief.

Devotee

I move on like the
winds over the ocean
a force to be reckoned with—
but I've made mistakes with
my devotion
devils breath arranged within closed fist.

Constellation

On what rooftop
do we lay our heads and listen
to the thrum of the life within?

Is it delusion yet
to feel the heartbeat of Orion
pulsating in the night sky?

And, then, what to make of it?
if we are exposing
the sides of the moon which have no face?

I have tasted the mirror
to find flavorful lies
within a ghastly reflection

And found, thus far,
that shards of silver are much
more enticing to the palate.

Matter

Is an offering of deep solace
not enough?
or does it simply always take
blood to
close the deal?
I myself, at times,
am an offering
of flesh and bone,
heart and soil.

Where does that leave me?
I matter,
on occasion,
usually when
necessary.

Other times, the night creeps in
and I am exposed prey
without very much meat
on my bones.

*B*roken Glass

Fingertips gripping marble,
I can't remember what I was wearing.
as the sun emerged it glazed the hills
with the spoils of glimmering
yellow and orange.
I simply woke up,
still drunk on moon beams
and broken glass
I wondered if I would keep
this memory,
or if it would pour out of
my ears into the wind
and be carried away—
that would be mercy.

*H*ere It Is

I know for a fact that you couldn't love me how you
may want to—
and I feel uncomfortable that you would even
imagine that you could.
You knew that it would be selfish to drag me into
your pain—
and smother me with it so that it could kill someone
other than you.
Maybe if you had asked, I would feel different,
but I think that's just as unlikely.
Could you not imagine that perhaps
the drink could not actually keep you
as warm as you wanted it to?

Stains

You were a stain
on my lips—

while I was a stain
on your teeth.

Four Corners

If only the road would hold still,
the rain would shift evenly to the corners of
the cardinal directions
and fill the bowls of those who wait.
Southern chalice of hope for those who
are stuck and striving to be who the world
around them wishes they weren't,
northern sepulcher filled to the brim with secret
venom
and stoicism rampant
westerly jar overflowing with those who
own land which can never be their own
the east that moves within itself—
up and down, stirred with old bitterness.

Change

Rebirth after
loss,
a significant
key
to becoming
new—
the cycle
rapidly
closes in,
I am not
afraid
to change.

Celestial

Look at the way the universe spins
for you—
A silent cacophony of celestial beings,
holy bodies,
they are magnetic—
drawn to the center.

Such is the way of the sky,
bound by physics and
that which cannot be seen—
the center becomes what it is not,
a love affair burning to begin.

Third Act

The flames taste like autumn and smoke
like catharsis that flutters into the sky
a cloudy start on a day marked by
conflagration.

It doesn't end with sadness,
or kindness, even softer—
sanctity is fueled by a tranquility
unattainable.

*P*ractice

Instability

yields

creativity,

be

mindful

of your

ghosts.

Round

Must we have
this cyclical venture
on every path we take?

The end is the beginning—
the beginning the end,
and nowhere in between
lives our destination.

It is a misfortune
I would rather not partake in.

I'll Wait

Why make enemies
with the spirit of fortune?
If all you gain is a fear of the unknown,
a wasted curiosity you'll be.

I'd send a token of
rosemary, lilac—
though the meaning would be lost
if you weren't to
follow through.

Be as you will, if you'd like,
unafraid and emboldened,
I will continue to light
lanterns
on your
path.

Endings

The boys lend a hand in the field,
the docks sway rapidly by the sea—
each world we live in is designed
for us to build and breathe.

The elderly clasp their swollen joints,
no pain in love, but the body withers—
the end will not creep up or move,
a mercy until the close of winter.

*B*rine

I always feel like I'm wading through brackish water
a little white water, fierce current—
and my thin, spindly fingers can't compress
against the tide
that the gales still lovingly abide.

Am I underneath? Is it colder still?
Will the water really cleanse me, as my mother says that it
will?
I'm soaking up all the mud, just like a sponge—
but my body is still stiff and with the rudders I still lunge

for the open, deep, and for my heart that
always beats, just a little out of time—
it makes a delicate old home out of the
underlying brine.

Part IV
Hiems

Restful

Waft to me
a smell so sweet
as victory.

Where the soles of our shoes
meet the bottoms of our feet,
there our spirts will learn the time to retreat.

There you'll find me,
all alone,
a song as burdensome as beckoning
still stale on my tongue.

And nothing more can be said—
nothing less can be heard,
than the souls sweet final call to
everlasting rest.

Wide

Blackened starlight,
the universe is an open,
empty mouth.

Dampened barrier,
the sound of the void is a
ticking clock.

*R*elease

Untie your knots
if you are tethered
to someone as bright
as the sun.

It is far better
to feel the touch of chill
than to try to heal
from deep, primal burns.

Fallen Underneath

Until the oil smothered the flame,
we gave way to heavy ships on the sea.
we had fallen underneath the waves,
where the light does not yet shine,
and we were content to be
submerged.

The Dog

I stumble each evening
from a creaky porch
to the old lands.

Once, fire fell and
ate up the flora
like golden honey on ripe tapioca.

Now the shell seems empty,
but is loaded
with spirits.

Like that of the dog—
perched under the bridge
who waits just for me.

The dog—
not always there,
and yet forever watching.

One day, I will bring him a bone
and hope
it is to his liking.

I dare not offend the dog under the bridge
for one day,
I will be perched with him.

As once, fire fell and
ate up the flora
like golden honey on ripe tapioca.

Finality

No rope could fray
like the end of a
winters night.

There are splinters
under his nails
while he guts
the fish.

We eat, breathe in
flames,
stars crash
out of the sky.

The end is only as romantic
as you make it.

Castle

Sweetness like honey,
spun like gold.
down the corridor,
but left out in the cold.

Doorways left open,
hallow columns hold the frame.
wet matchsticks and broken lamps
will always give way to the flame.

*S*easonal Death

I had once indulged
in sunshine and warmth
as though it were my defaulted
home.
A razors edge could not
have split me from
the rays of summers
embrace,
but now the winter finds it is
time to wrap its frozen
fingers around my
wrists.
It's nothing I have not
felt before, though
shocking as it may be—
I have accepted the
snow covered fields
to be my permanent
residency.

There are antlers on the ground,
the velvet peeling away,
any other time I might would expect
the summer, any day.
But this season is new to me,
and everything is strange.
I have come to terms,
seated on the ground,
that this world may
no longer age.

Untouched

Twisted, wrought iron cross
weathered and oxidized
guarding a golden sepulcher
touched by
gazing eyes,
and yet never with
finger tips.

This is the gospel
of tradition,
prioritizing righteous
sedition,
in an avenue leading
ash and cedar smoke
to fill young lungs.

We must not make
the wild mistake
of building
our confessional cot
to be
the lining of a
pale pine box.

*B*ecoming

We are not your image
of us
we have not yet become
anchors,
obliged to weigh down
the ether.

To Be Different

Is there nothing more than a cool embrace
to ritualize this moment?
I was already shivering—
could already see my breath.

Just once, if it could be warm
would we thaw, or melt like ice
to become something other
than ourselves?

Which of these is more
tantalizing—
to feel the heat and be the same,
or to become something else entirely?

$\mathcal{D}$ust

Understandably, I am tired of translucent
martyrdom, and have been
since a child.
The beiges of a day grown
to maturity and beyond
are nothing more than
a tan silhouette,
hiding behind a frame of dust.

Add Some Sugar

I was young—
there is not much else to say but at times,
I could not have known better, and no one could have,
with nothing to compare.
Concrete sidewalks grow wider and rougher
and the land between knowing and wanting
becomes dry,
and sometimes I feel like I'm chasing the pain away,
but really, I'm just chasing the pain—
no matter, the world grows sweeter with age and yet
somehow maintains its bitter aftertaste for those
who might would consider themselves
amateur sommeliers.
One dry glass of wine and a drop of French honey
to lighten the mood—
there are yet so many tools to convince yourself
that there is nothing in this world that
could possibly be bitter.

Smallness

Ill-fitting dress—
sheer and torn.
Dirty blue feet
that can weather
the storm,
A tiny pale creature she is.
rose stained and fair,
with rope in her hair—
indeed, a tiny pale creature she is.

Frost

Birds in the trees,
palatable misfortune,
summer covers spring like
a coat of down—
I have tasted the end of the
cold.

Not deeply, however,
as spindly threads tie
the seasons together,
and it's difficult to
tell one
from the other.

The ice does not find
its home in the hills
nor the valleys of
the foothills below—
not any more, at least.

Something Better to Come

For once I have seen
the world
as the anchor tethering
me to the universe—
a collision of sand
and crystal
became birth.

And for once I have seen
the universe
it is naked,
and it is bruised—
it is bound to our skin
and it is the script
for overture.

Comfortability

I am a mask,
and a shell
of the past,
growing with restlessness—
I am home.

What Is Done Is Done

Wilted flowers, begging the vicar
to give holy rights,
a proper burial
back to the soil they were
plucked from—
their birth right
became death right,
and they are not afraid
except to not be returned.

Curling

Meet me where the rain is sour
where the divide is all but amiss—
the foundation for our eternal
spirit is aflame, unburdened,
bliss.

You're not the first spirit to unfold
amongst the curling vines of ivy—
I cherish your presence until it withers,
this is the path we chose,
untimely.

$\mathscr{A}$ Connection

Visceral
Your body is a
vessel
to carry your thoughts and
your persuasions,
your gifts
for special occasions—
a temple expected
to be
demolished
and rebuilt
into something or
another
that is more,
or perhaps even less,
but still
as important.
Your body is
eternal—
in some form,
you carry energy
from
ages beforehand—
does it feel
familiar?

*K*nots

Rest deep and rest long,
your breath a steady cadence
to an unending song,
it's only a change—
only a knot in the wood,
more character to love,
which, reasonably,
you understood.

Grave

Against the sunset, the glinting snow
melts brightly, dripping down old stone,
the catalyst for change is not held within
the lives whose shells remain bound to the earth,
their places in time relevant only to our
own.

Again—it is possible, if not probable,
that the earth between our toes is comprised of
broken bones which belonged to us at one point,
and then, as always, no longer belonged to us
but to the gods that pedestal themselves upon our
perches.

The wrens and crows which follow the bleached stones
know the actuality of this space—that which is gone
can never be definitively gone,
and, truthfully, that which became
can never become
undone.

Moving Along

Sage green,
essence of the ghosts we have yet
to become—the loftiness wears on our mouths
and threatens to dilute our words of abundance.
If ever there were a time that graciousness and
modern civility would come to pass—
well, I don't know, we
have not gotten there just yet.
I will only take this one breath as sacred
and untainted by those who applaud our
unhappiness—
but then, after that, I suppose we should move on.

Merlot

Gemstone
and shards of porcelain plates littering the front yard
merlot painted nostalgia and for the life of me,
I can't remember it like I'd like to—
but the flavor lingers in the creases of my cheeks
where a smile, or frown,
would squeeze it out and onto my rosy tongue,
aromatic.

Perhaps

From what loom should we consider god to have been
woven
upon—
or any creature here below with sinew and fiber,
with blood rolling through arteries and a solid
body?
Should the last of all grasps for reality be taken
by a vision of unsurmountable mountain range,
well, I think that would be okay.
At least beautiful, if nothing else—
and isn't that what we have been striving for, anyway?
each ever growing distance between ourselves and
something beautiful—
something lovely.
Well, yes, I think that would be okay.

*Y*et Another

Look at what we're calling love
take a glance between, deep in the spaces unnerved—
should we lose yet another war? I have seen too much
failure in myself to wish it upon any other,
but should you fail,
take it in with reverence.

www.ingramcontent.com/pod-product-compliance
Lightning Source LLC
Chambersburg PA
CBHW060031050426
42448CB00012B/2955